The
That Changed A Life

MATTHEW 13:45-46 FOR CHILDREN

Written by Judy Lund

Illustrated by Vaccaro Associates

ARCH Books

COPYRIGHT © 1970 BY CONCORDIA PUBLISHING HOUSE,
    ST. LOUIS, MISSOURI
CONCORDIA PUBLISHING HOUSE LTD., LONDON, E. C. 1
MANUFACTURED IN THE UNITED STATES OF AMERICA
ALL RIGHTS RESERVED
ISBN 0-570-06049-4

Abu El Akbar, it is said,
was the richest man in the land.
His billowing robes were golden,
fine jewels adorned each hand.

One so rich should be happy and gay,
but Abu El Akbar? Oh, no!

He spent his days in wandering,
searching high and low,
asking of every friend and foe,
"Where is the pearl of great price?"

He climbed the lofty mountaintop
and crossed the driest plain;

he searched the deepest valley,
but his efforts were in vain.

Into the steaming jungles he trod,
prepared for any test.
His shoulders drooped, his body ached,
but he would never rest.
He had to try his very best
to find the pearl of great price.

He followed a sparkling, silver brook
till it joined the ocean's roar
in a thundering falls of laughing foam;
he'd not been here before.

He stood and gazed at the view below
until it was nearly night,
and then, across the blue-green bay,
he spied a city's light.
He felt this place would be just right
to find the pearl of great price.

He eagerly ran through the city streets,
searching shop after shop.
But finding nothing, he sighed, discouraged,
"Will my search ever stop?"

He sat on the ground, his head in his hands;
he couldn't go on, he feared.

Then he heard the sound of a tapping cane
as a bearded old stranger neared.
He stopped—in his outstretched hand appeared
the perfect pearl of great price.

Abu looked at the pearl and blinked his eyes
once and twice and then thrice.
"How much must I pay for this pearl?" he asked,
"It's worth any sacrifice."

The bearded one spoke very soft and slow.
He said, "The only way
is to sell all you own, every grain, every thread,
and on that very day
bring all to me, and then you may
own the pearl of great price."

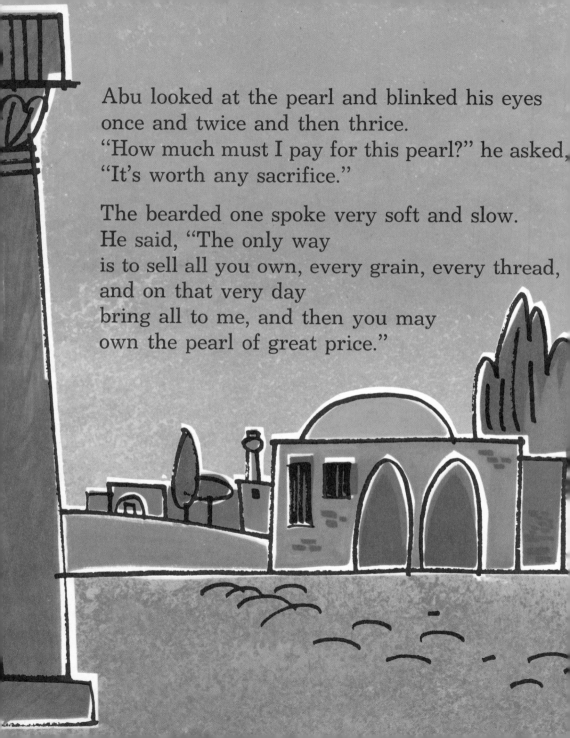

He eagerly thanked the old stranger, and then he hurried to sell all he owned.
His neighbors watched and shook their heads. "He must be mad," they moaned.

He sold his house, his lands, his books, the carpets in every hall.

He sold his bird and its golden cage
and his horse so strong and tall.
He didn't regret his decision at all
to gain the pearl of great price.

He packed the gold in a leather bag
to pay for the pearl he desired.
He found the man and gave him the bag
with the gold that he had acquired.

At last he had the perfect pearl,
and he sang and danced with joy.
The old one smiled and said to him,
"You'll not want nor weep, my boy.
From this day on you will enjoy
your perfect pearl of great price."

DEAR PARENTS:

Our interesting story is an expanded version of Jesus' kingdom parable in Matthew 13:45-46. The description of the merchant in search of fine pearls, of his discovery of the most valuable pearl, and of his actions to acquire the pearl of great price heighten the drama of the story. The point is that when he found the Pearl of Great Price he concentrated all his efforts on obtaining it. He sold all he had to gain the one pearl of greatest value. It was the pearl that changed his life.

As the merchant in the parable, we are led to make the great and surprising discovery that the most valuable pearl is the Good News of forgiveness and new life in Jesus Christ. The effect of discovering this joyful news is overpowering. We leave all other interests behind and concentrate on the one goal of living the new life of Christ under His gracious rule.

Have you discovered the Pearl of Great Price that changes lives? Money, honor, popularity, power, material things fade away as goals in life when we come to faith in Christ. Give your child the best gift of all. Help him set his goal to live in the love of Christ.

THE EDITOR

Reading together is fun with
SHARE-A-STORY

A series specially designed to help you encourage your child to read. The right and left-hand pages are arranged so that you take turns and the story develops as a conversation. Fresh, humorous stories illustrated by top artists ensure enjoyment for everyone!

'Revolutionary . . . done with as much good psychology as good humour . . . Pat Thomson has contrived a set of readers likely to brighten bedtime for all parties' — *Mail on Sunday*

NO TROUBLE
AT ALL

by

Pat Thomson

Illustrated by

Jocelyn Wild

PUFFIN BOOKS

Auntie, it's me. I'm home.
Mum told me you would be here
looking after Susie.
Was she good?

She was a little pet.
No trouble at all.
She's in bed now,
fast asleep.

That makes a change.
She's up to mischief most days.
Was she really good?

Of course she was, dear.
She was eating her breakfast
when I arrived.
There was a lot of breakfast
on the cat,
but that was an accident.

The cat's used to it.
Did you wash her next?
You didn't leave her
at the sink, did you?

Funny you should say that.
"Wash your hands, pet," I said.
Next time I turned round
the cat was swimming for its life.

That cleaned him up.
The floor looks clean, too.
Susie likes playing with water.

Yes, she had a lovely time.
She was playing boats.
I just wish she hadn't
sailed her shoes.

She's full of ideas.
Sometimes she's a good helper.
Did she help you?

Oh certainly.
She tidied up the bedrooms.
She threw everyone's underwear
over the fence.
That was a bit awkward.

That's dreadful.
Did anyone see?
I'm glad I was at school.

Susie tries to be useful.
She said her buggy squeaked
so she oiled it with syrup.

I wondered why the cat
was licking it.
Mum lets her make pastry.
That keeps her busy.

I know.
She made a sweet pastry hat
for the cat.

Oh no!
I don't think she's been good at all.
It was one of her funny days.

Nonsense, dear.
She painted me a lovely picture.
It was all green and yellow.
Is Teddy washable, by the way?

Poor old Teddy!
She painted him as well.
Green and yellow stripes!
He looks like a caterpillar.

She was very lively today,
so I took her to the park.
She barked at a fierce dog.

I hope she didn't bite it.
She's fierce as well.

Of course she isn't.
She walked home very nicely.
I let her post my letters.
Pity she posted them
down the drain.

Oh dear.
Susie always does that.
I should have warned you.

She played in the garden
for a while.
I kept a close eye on her.
I can't think how she buried
the cat's dinner.
Lucky he found it.

She had a busy day!
You had a busy day, too.
Even the *cat* had a busy day.

I enjoyed every minute.
It reminds me of the times
I used to babysit for you.

Was I like that?
No wonder Mum needs
a day off now and then!
Is that her coming now?

Yes, here she is.
Everything's fine, dear.
The baby was a little pet.
No trouble at all.

PUFFIN BOOKS

Published by the Penguin Group
Penguin Books Ltd, 27 Wrights Lane, London W8 5TZ, England
Penguin Putnam Inc., 375 Hudson Street, New York, New York 10014, USA
Penguin Books Australia Ltd, Ringwood, Victoria, Australia
Penguin Books Canada Ltd, 10 Alcorn Avenue, Toronto, Ontario, Canada M4V 3B2
Penguin Books (NZ) Ltd, Private Bag 102902, NSMC, Auckland, New Zealand

Penguin Books Ltd, Registered Offices: Harmondsworth, Middlesex, England

First published by Victor Gollancz Ltd 1989
Published in Gollancz Children's Paperbacks 1995
Published in Puffin Books 1998
5 7 9 10 8 6 4

Text copyright © Pat Thomson, 1989
Illustrations copyright © Jocelyn Wild, 1989
All rights reserved

Printed in Hong Kong by Wing King Tong Co. Ltd

British Library Cataloguing in Publication Data
A CIP catalogue record for this book is available from the British Library

ISBN 0-140-38883-4

Other *Share-A-Story* titles

BEST PEST
Pat Thomson and Peter Firmin

THE BEST THING OF ALL
Pat Thomson and Margaret Chamberlain

CAN YOU HEAR ME, GRANDAD?
Pat Thomson and Jez Alborough

DIAL D FOR DISASTER
Pat Thomson and Paul Demeyer

GOOD GIRL GRANNY
Pat Thomson and Faith Jaques

MY FRIEND MR MORRIS
Pat Thomson and Satoshi Kitamura

NO TROUBLE AT ALL
Pat Thomson and Jocelyn Wild

ONE OF THOSE DAYS
Pat Thomson and Bob Wilson

THE TREASURE SOCK
Pat Thomson and Tony Ross